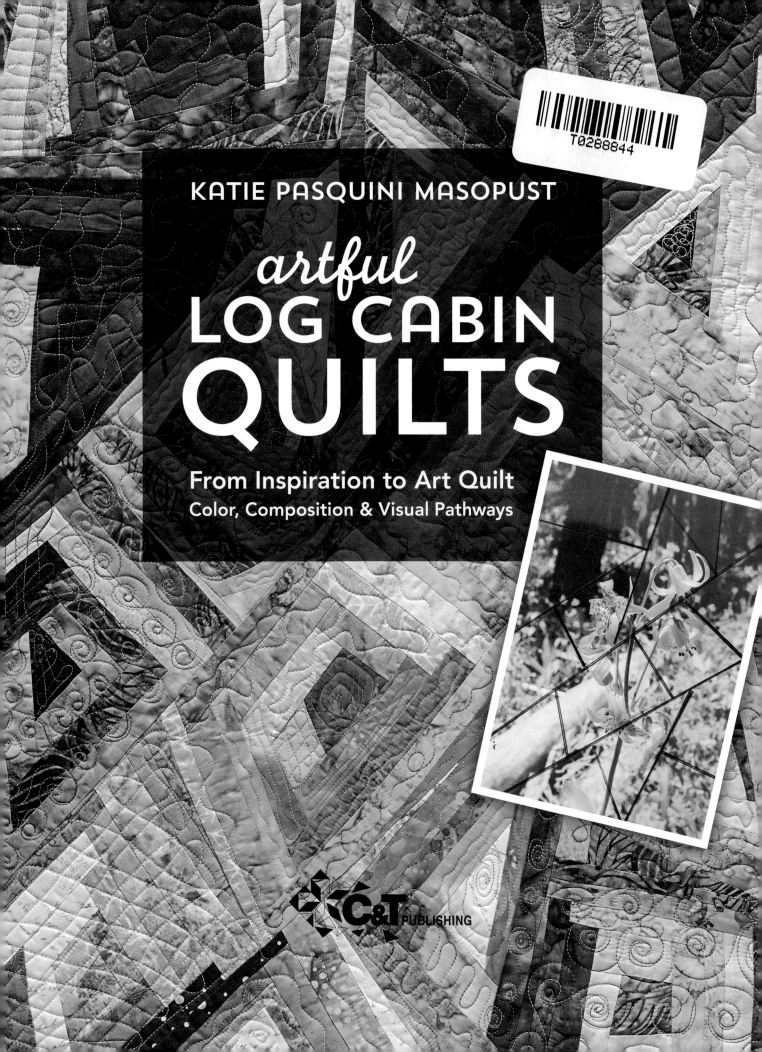

KATIE PASQUINI MASOPUST

artful LOG CABIN QUILTS

From Inspiration to Art Quilt
Color, Composition & Visual Pathways

C&T PUBLISHING

Publisher: Amy Marson

Creative Director: Gailen Runge

Editor: Lynn Koolish

Technical Editor: Susan Nelsen

Cover/Book Designer: April Mostek

Production Coordinator: Joe Edge

Production Editor: Jennifer Warren

Illustrator: Valyrie Gillum

Photo Assistants: Carly Jean Marin and Mai Yong Vang

Instructional photography by Diane Pedersen of C&T Publishing, Inc., unless otherwise noted

Published by C&T Publishing, Inc., P.O. Box 1456, Lafayette, CA 94549

Library of Congress Cataloging-in-Publication Data

Names: Pasquini Masopust, Katie, author.

Title: Artful log cabin quilts : from inspiration to art quilt - color, composition & visual pathways / Katie Pasquini Masopust.

Description: Lafayette, CA : C&T Publishing, Inc., 2017.

Identifiers: LCCN 2016042393 | ISBN 9781617454509 (soft cover)

Subjects: LCSH: Quilting--Technique. | Log cabin quilts. | Art quilts.

Classification: LCC TT835 .P3655 2017 | DDC 746.46--dc23

LC record available at https://lccn.loc.gov/2016042393

Printed in the USA

10 9 8 7 6 5 4 3

DEDICATION

To Cindy Barfield, my faithful assistant and friend. Thank you for everything you do for me.

To Sandy Chapin, for inspiring me.

Thanks to my sewing buddy, Jody, for taking the time to make Artful Log Cabins with me.

To my editor, Lynn Koolish, for her keen eye and excellent words.

To my husband, for his infinite patience about everything!

And to my California "family"—Randalyn, Holly, and Terrie. I love you all so much!

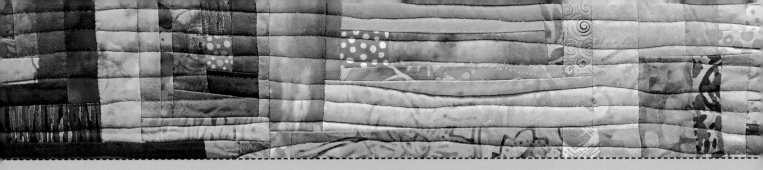

CONTENTS

HISTORY OF THE
ARTFUL LOG CABIN

TRADITIONAL LOG CABIN QUILTS

I love Log Cabin quilts, and I have been making them for more than 30 years. I enjoy the way the lights and darks play off each other and the hundreds of different patterns that can be created when all the blocks are put together.

The traditional Log Cabin block usually has a red center square to symbolize the fire in the hearth and the warmth of a log cabin home. The majority of the block is made up of strips of the same width in light and dark values.

Barn Raising (for Larry and Sheryl Pasquini) by Katie Pasquini Masopust, Holly Cunningham, and Terrie Pasquini Robertson; 100″ × 100″; 2014

Photo by Carolyn Wright

Construction of the block starts with the center square. Strips are added in a clockwise manner, starting with two light strips on two adjacent sides of the center block. These light strips symbolize the sides of the cabin that are brightened by the sun.

Next, two dark strips are added to the two remaining sides of the center block. These strips symbolize the shadowed sides of the cabin.

This pattern is carried out until the block reaches its finished size. Generally, three strips per side will create the preferred patterns, but more strips can be added to make the block the desired size.

Red square with two light strips

Two dark strips added

Completed block

making traditional log cabin quilts

The Twisted Scissor Sisters Log Cabin Quilters
2015 Patriotic Sew-a-Thon

Photo by Sarah Chapman and Katie Pasquini Masopust

My sisters and I get together at least twice a year to make Log Cabin quilts. During one of these visits, we make bed-size traditional Log Cabins for ourselves or loved ones. In May, over the long Memorial Day weekend, we make red, white, and blue patriotic quilts to honor our veterans and to thank them for all that they do for us. We donate our quilts to the veterans program at College of the Redwoods in Humboldt County, California, where one of my sisters works.

MY TRADITIONAL LOG CABIN QUILTS

I have made many traditional Log Cabin quilts over the years and love every minute of it.

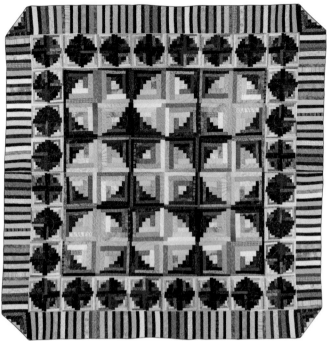

Circular Log Cabin by Katie Pasquini Masopust, 98″ × 97″, 2011

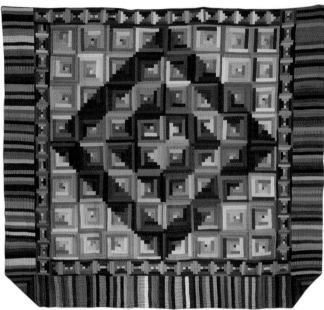

Custom Log Cabin by Katie Pasquini Masopust, 100″ × 97″, 2009

Barn Raising with Accents (for Randalyn Perkins) by Katie Pasquini Masopust, 98″ × 98″, 2013

Mark's Quilt by Katie Pasquini Masopust, Holly Cunningham, and Terrie Pasquini Robertson; 100″ × 100″; 2016

Photo by Katie Pasquini Masopust

Straight Furrows Log Cabin (for Bobby Masopust Jr.) by Katie Pasquini Masopust, 56″ × 104″, 2014

Photos by Carolyn Wright

ARTFUL LOG CABIN QUILTS

I teach my designs and techniques throughout the world. Periodically I have to create new classes so I can keep returning to my favorite venues. During one of these times, I realized that I love making Log Cabin quilts but had never taught them.

If I was going to teach Log Cabin quilts, I had to put a new spin on this traditional design. What if I made it more abstract? I could add different types of grids to the traditional perpendicular grid. Beautiful places and objects are such an inspiration to me—could I use photographs to inspire the colors and values for the Log Cabin? Now I had the beginning of a great new class!

The new grids would be placed over a photograph, and each block would be made up of the colors and the values seen in that portion of the photo. All forms would be reduced to lines of color (the lines being the strips of fabric making up the Log Cabin), creating a strong abstract design.

My new class became Artful Log Cabins, and I am now sharing it with you. I hope you enjoy it as much as I do! Happy Creating!

INSPIRATIONAL
PHOTOGRAPHS

The first step in creating an Artful Log Cabin is to choose an inspiration. Most often this is a photograph, but some may choose to use a painting.

The inspirational photograph or painting can be of any subject matter that excites you. Keep in mind that the quilt will not look exactly like the image; instead, it will be inspired by the colors and composition of the photograph or painting for a more abstract Log Cabin quilt.

COMPOSITION

The inspirational image should have a good composition—that is, the way the objects or colors are arranged within the frame. The chart (next page) shows some of the more common compositional layouts that quilters find in their images and use in their quilts.

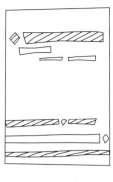

Horizontal

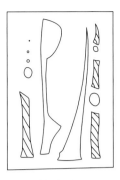

Vertical

Diagonal

Radiating

Circular

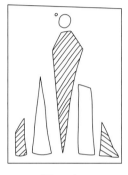

Triangular

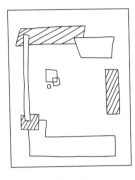

Framed

Vanishing

Grid

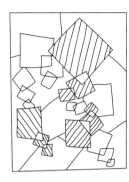

Overall

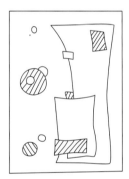

Asymmetrical

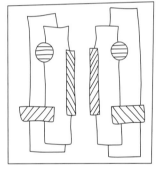

Symmetrical

Cruciform

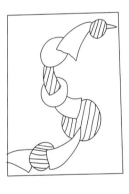

S Curve

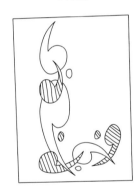

L Form

Horizontal: strong horizontal placement and movement of the forms and/or colors

Vertical: strong vertical placement and movement of the forms and/or colors

Diagonal: forms and/or colors placed diagonally through the piece

Radiating: forms and/or colors densely placed in one area that then radiate to the outer edges in a more open placement

Circular: dominant forms and/or colors placed to move the eye in a large circle through the piece

Triangular: forms and/or colors placed to create a triangle through the piece

Framed: a border of forms and/or colors that frames the focal point

Vanishing: larger forms and/or colors in the foreground get smaller as they recede in the distance

Grid: a combination of horizontal and vertical forms and/or colors

Overall: no definite composition but a balance of colors and/or forms throughout the piece

Asymmetrical: uneven placement of forms and/or colors on either side of a centerline

Symmetrical: even, balanced placement of forms and/or colors on either side of a centerline

Cruciform: forms and/or colors that create a cross within the piece

S Curve: an S-like pathway through the piece created by the placement of the forms and/or colors

L Form: forms and/or colors that make a strong L shape, framing a secondary area

WHAT IS A GOOD PHOTOGRAPH?

Your inspirational image should have a good composition and colors that you want to use. Squint your eyes at the photograph to make sure you like the layout of the colors and values. The placement of the colors and values should set up a visual pathway through the piece—meaning they should lead the eye through the piece so the viewer can explore the whole design. Photos with too much color everywhere or fine details of color separations will be less successful. Below are some examples of good photographs that can be used with this technique.

Radiating composition: Three separate color areas (rusty orange for the bricks, red-orange for the flowers, and green for the leaves that radiate up from the bottom of the photo) create a radiating visual pathway up through the image.

S-curve composition: Multiple colors move through the greens.

S-curve composition: Reds and oranges move through the greens, creating an S-shaped visual pathway through the piece.

Photos by Katie
Pasquini Masopust

Horizontal composition: Horizontal bands of colors and values create a horizontal pathway, which keeps the eye moving back and forth through the piece.

POOR PHOTOGRAPHS AND HOW TO IMPROVE THEM

Poor photographs can often be improved by cropping to create a stronger composition. A cropper, made from a mat for framing pictures, is a very handy tool. Cut the mat on two opposite corners to create two L shapes. Place these over the photograph and move them around until you discover a strong composition.

Following are some examples of how to use cropping to strengthen the composition, the proportions of color, or both.

Use a cropper to find a strong composition.

In this photo, one color is dominated by medium values.

Crop the photo to make a vertical format, bringing out more darks and focusing on the bit of yellow to create an accent. The composition is now an S curve, which creates a visual pathway through the little plants.

In this photo, areas of color are not defined, and there are no large blocks of color or value.

The white flower is right in the middle of the photo, which would create a bull's-eye effect in the quilt.

Crop the photo to create an asymmetrical composition, with the flower filling the lower right side and accents of white spreading across the top. Once cropped, the violet in the background appears, adding a nice accent to the white and green color scheme.

Crop the photo to make a vertical format, emphasizing the feeling of trees growing and focusing in on the green and yellow leaves that now dominate the composition. The composition is now diagonal and creates a visual pathway from the lower right to the upper left.

In this photo, the large red flower is in the center, and the green is in equal amounts all around.

Crop out some of the green to create an asymmetrical composition and to allow the red to dominate. The visual pathway could move around the flower, then out to the red bud, then around and up to the unopened bud, creating a circular pathway.

In this photo, the flower is in the middle of the composition. This image would be difficult to crop and make more interesting; don't use this type of photo.

Use this type of photo instead. The big flower is off-center and is balanced by the smaller one, creating an asymmetrical composition with a visual pathway that moves back and forth between the two flowers.

In this photo, multiple flowers move the eye around the piece, with the three large flower centers creating a triangular composition.

In this photo, there is too much of the same color, and there aren't enough differences in color and value. Don't use this type of photo.

Photos by Katie Pasquini Masopust

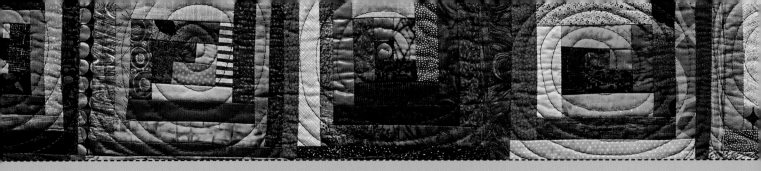

GRIDS

A grid breaks an image into units that will become the Log Cabin blocks, and many different types of grids can be used. Read through this discussion of the different grids before selecting a grid for your project. The more you explore the grids, the more ideas you will come up with to create the perfect grid for your particular inspiration.

EVEN PERPENDICULAR GRID

Even perpendicular grids have horizontal and vertical lines perpendicular to each other and are made with even spacing between all the lines.

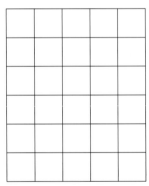

Even perpendicular grid

Even perpendicular grid on a photo of a cactus

Inspiration photo by Katie Pasquini Masopust

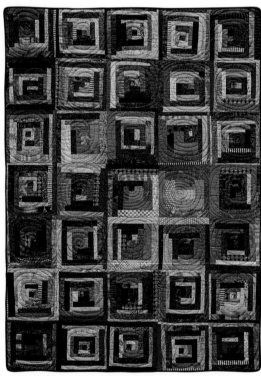

Cactus by Katie Pasquini Masopust, 30″ × 42″, 2015

Even perpendicular grid: blocks made using strips of various widths

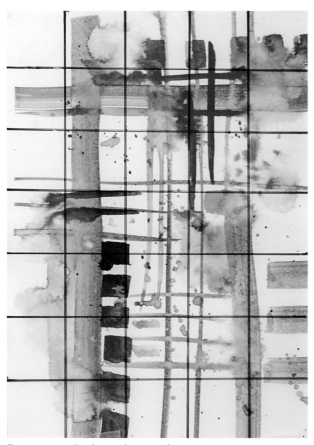

Even perpendicular grid on an abstract painting

Abstract inspiration painting by Katie Pasquini Masopust

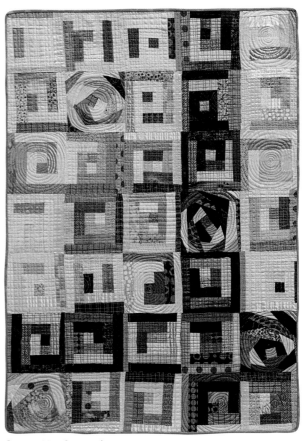

Spring Has Sprung by Katie Pasquini Masopust, 35˝ × 26˝, 2016

Even perpendicular grid: blocks made using strips of the same width

EVEN DIAGONAL GRID

Even perpendicular grids placed on the diagonal achieve a different look.

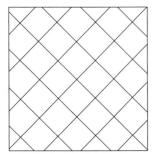

Even diagonal grid

Even diagonal grid on a photo of poppies

Inspiration photo by Katie Pasquini Masopust

Poppies by Katie Pasquini Masopust,
28″ × 21″, 2016

Even diagonal grid: blocks made using strips of the same width

DIAMOND GRID

A diamond grid is created by moving the diagonal grid lines slightly off the perpendicular.

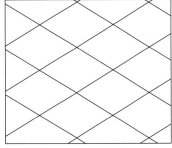

Diamond grid

Diamond grid on a photo of Hawaiian flowers

Inspiration photo by Terri Pasquini Robertson

Hawaii by Terri Pasquini Robertson, 27″ × 17″, 2016

Diamond grid: blocks made using strips of the same width

Diamond grid on a painting of tulips

Inspiration painting by Judith Ritner

Pachelbel's Tulips by Judith Ritner, 19″ × 38″, 2016

Diamond grid: blocks made using strips of the same width

RANDOM GRID

Random grids have uneven distances between the perpendicular and/or diagonal lines.

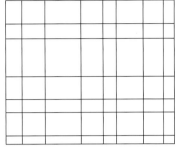

Random grid

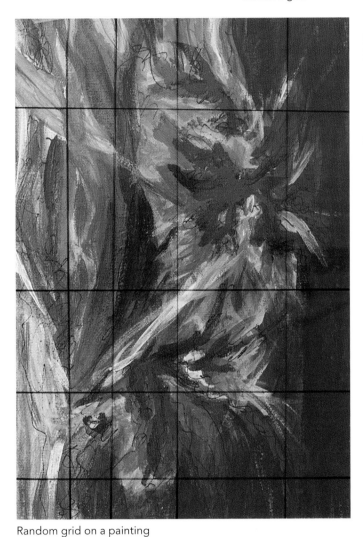

Random grid on a painting

Inspiration painting by Jody L. DeCoursin-Good

Sunset Orchid by Jody L. DeCoursin-Good, 19″ × 28″, 2015

Random grid: blocks made using strips of the same width

Random grid on a photo of a bird-of-paradise flower

Inspiration photo by Margie Bushaw

Beach Paradise by Margie Bushaw, 23″ × 29″, 2016

Random grid: blocks made using strips of various widths

Random grid on a photo of a landscape

Inspiration photo by Mary Mattimoe

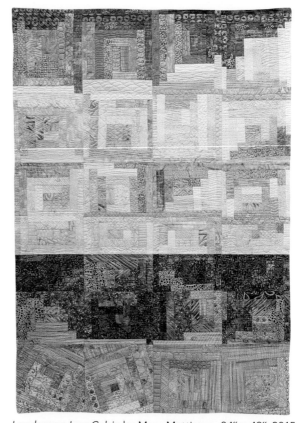

Landscape Log Cabin by Mary Mattimoe, 34″ × 49″, 2015

Random grid: blocks made using strips of the same width

OPEN GRID

Lines can be erased from the grid to create some very large squares for an open grid.

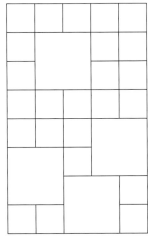

Open grid

Open grid on a photo of bromeliads

Inspiration photo by Katie Pasquini Masopust

Bromeliad by Katie Pasquini Masopust, 32˝ × 20˝, 2015

Open grid: blocks made using strips of the same width

VARIABLE GRID

A variable grid is created by breaking up some of the squares into smaller squares, rectangles, or even triangles.

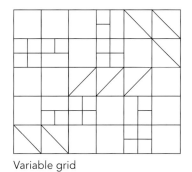

Variable grid

Variable grid drawn to match a photo of *The Etretat Cliffs after the Storm*, a painting by Gustave Courbet

Inspiration photo courtesy of WikiMedia Commons

Inspiration by Ruth A. Moran, 27″ × 37″, 2016

Variable grid: blocks made using strips of various widths

Variable grid on a photo of a fishing village on the island of Chiloé, Chile

Inspiration photo by Jan Whitehead

Fishing Village by Annelies Massey, quilted by Joy Hegglund, 31″ × 24″, 2016

Variable grid: blocks made using strips of various widths

Variable grid on a photo of Swiss chard

Inspiration photo by Anita Marsh McSorley

Swiss Chard on Blue Plate by Anita Marsh McSorley, 42″ × 32″, 2016

Variable grid: blocks made using strips of various widths

Variable grid on a photo of red claret cup cactus and purple scorpionweed

Inspiration photo by Lynn Rogers

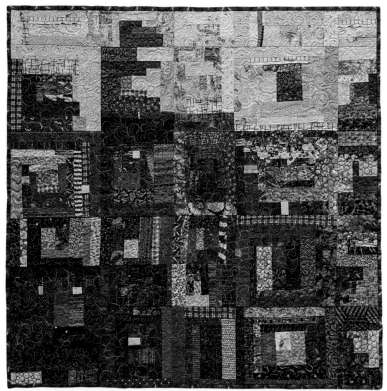

Natives in the Cabin by Lynn Rogers, 25″ × 25″, 2015

Variable grid: blocks made using strips of various widths

WONKY GRID

A wonky grid is made by using nonperpendicular lines with uneven spacing.

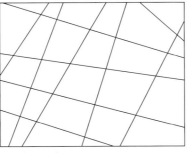

Wonky grid

Wonky grid on a photo of a rose in front of the Imagination! Pavilion at Epcot Theme Park

Inspiration photo by Alison Chandler-Johnson

Figment's Rose by Alison Chandler-Johnson, 36″ × 25″, 2015

Wonky grid: blocks made using strips of various widths

Wonky grid on a painting

Inspiration painting by Katie Pasquini Masopust

Artful Exploration by Holly Cunningham, 24″ × 22″, 2016

Wonky grid: blocks made using strips of the same width

Wonky grid on a photo of peppers

Inspiration photo by Kathy M. Kuhn

Artful Log Peppers by Judy A. Hunt, 24″ × 16″, 2015

Wonky grid: blocks made using strips of various widths

Wonky grid on a painting of horses

Inspiration painting by Gail Gash Taylor

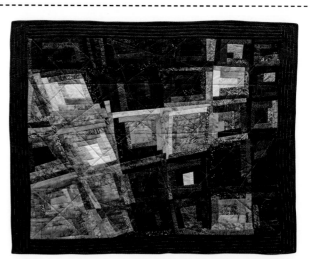

In Good Company by Maribelle Ogilvie, 38″ × 30″, 2016

Wonky grid: blocks made using strips of various widths

RADIATING GRID

Radiating grids have lines that radiate from one or more points.

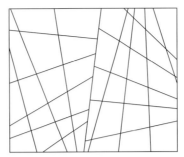

Radiating grid

Radiating grid on a photo of water lilies

Inspiration photo by Paula Ray

Lily with Bee by Paula Ray, 36″ × 24″, 2015

Radiating grid: blocks made using strips of the same width

Radiating grid on a close-up photo of a croton plant

Inspiration photo by Katie Pasquini Masopust

Explosion by Katie Pasquini Masopust, 32″ × 42″, 2016

Radiating grid: blocks made using strips of various widths

FRAMING GRID

A frame of radiating-grid Log Cabin blocks can be placed around a quilt center.

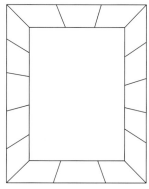

Framing grid

Serene Outlook on Life by Julia Graves, 26″ × 32″, 2015

Framing grid: radiating-grid blocks made using strips of various widths

COMBINING GRIDS

There's no reason why you can't combine grids.

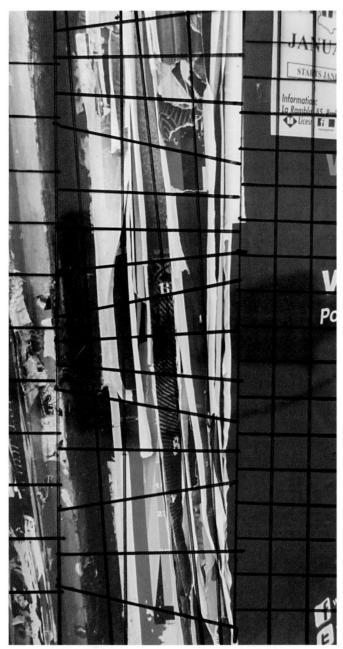

A combination of wonky and even perpendicular grids on a photo of posters stacked on a wall in Spain

Inspiration photo by Katie Pasquini Masopust

Poco a Poco—Little by Little by Katie Pasquini Masopust, 72″ × 38″, 2015

Wonky and even perpendicular grids: blocks made using strips of various widths

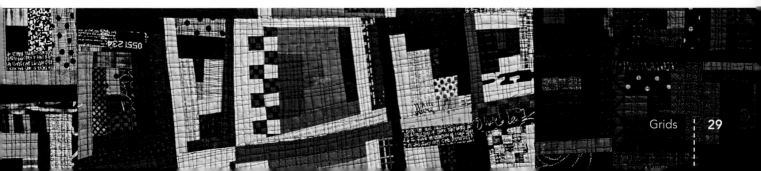

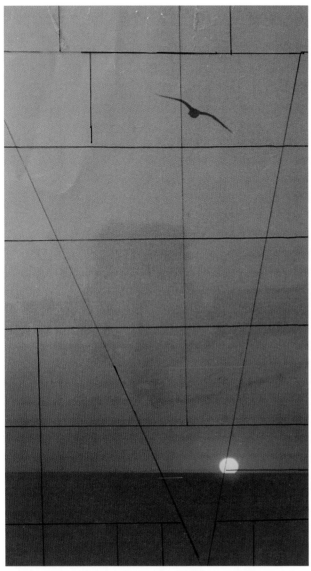

Combination of wonky and random grids on a photo of a sunset

Inspiration photo by Miriam Velazquez-Fagley

Sunset in Corsica by Miriam Velazquez-Fagley, 35″ × 23″, 2015

Wonky and random grids: blocks made using strips of the same width

Random and radiating grids on a photo of a bird-of-paradise

Inspiration photo by Mark J. Freitas

Paradise Abstracted by AnneMarie Freitas, 42″ × 34″, 2016

Random and radiating grids: blocks made using strips of various widths

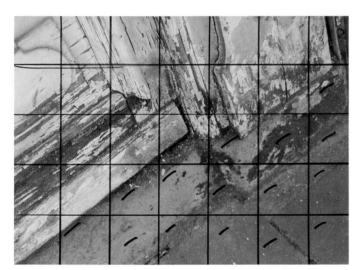

Even perpendicular grid with diagonal marks to indicate which blocks will be cut on the diagonal

Inspiration photo by Katie Pasquini Masopust

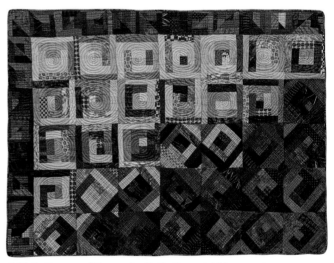

A Little Corner of France by Katie Pasquini Masopust, 30″ × 38″, 2016

Even perpendicular grid, with some blocks cut on the diagonal to match the direction in the photo: blocks made using strips of the same width

OTHER GRIDS

Anything goes for grids that can fit together. A very clever student
created a hexagon block for a unique look.

Elongated hexagon grid on a photo of fall foliage

Inspiration photo by Laurie Schierer

A *View from Home* by Laurie Schierer, 23″ × 27″, 2016

Hexagon grid: blocks made using strips of the same width

CHOOSING YOUR PROJECT GRID

The next step in this process is to choose a grid
to place over the photograph. Explore several of
the grid ideas using tracing paper, a ruler, and a
pencil.

1. Place tracing paper over the photograph and
use a ruler and pencil to create different grids.

2. Create at least 4 different possibilities to
loosen up; then focus on your favorite.

3. Draw your favorite several more times: the first
time to try to improve it, then again to simplify it,
and then once more to create the desired grid.

4. Draw your final grid with a permanent pen on
a piece of clear plastic or acetate to allow you to
see all the colors and values clearly.

FABRICS

USE A FULL RANGE OF VALUES

Good photographs will have a full range of values within them:

- Very light values where the sun is brightest or where the whites are white

- Medium values for the majority

- Very dark values for the shadows and the blacks

Photo with a full value range from light to dark in red, yellow, and green

When choosing your fabrics, match *all* the values in the photograph. If there is white in the photograph, you will want to use white in your fabrics. Gather all the values of the colors in the photograph—you can use solids, small prints, tone-on-tone, and large prints, as long as the fabric reads as one color and one value.

Having said that, some areas may have multiple colors. For example, you may want to find a print that includes all the colors of a grouping of small flowers or colorful feathers. Anything goes! Enjoy searching through your fabrics for many colors and values. No matter how much you have, you will always wish you had more, so don't be stingy with your selections.

It is important to have a full range of values from light to medium to dark. Color gets all the credit, but value does all the work.

A full value range of fabric from light to dark in the colors to match the photo: solids, large prints, and small prints, mostly tone-on-tones

Even perpendicular grid on a photo of dahlias

Inspiration photo by Jody L. DeCoursin-Good

Summer Dahlias by Jody L. DeCoursin-Good, 22″ × 30″, 2016

Even perpendicular grid: blocks made using strips of the same width

Random grid on a photo of lupine

Inspiration photo by Laura Reardon

Christmas in New Zealand by Laura Reardon, 29″ × 42″, 2016

Random grid: blocks made using strips of various widths

TYPES OF FABRICS AND FABRIC CONTENT

These quilts are meant to be hung as artwork and won't be cleaned as often as a bed quilt. Therefore, you can use any fabric content that you like. I like to use many different fiber contents, from cottons and blends to satins and corduroys to velveteen, and so on. They all reflect the light differently and add shimmer and excitement to the piece.

Open diagonal grid on a painting of an orchid

Inspiration painting by Pam Calderwood

Orchid by Pam Calderwood, 27″ × 37″, 2016

Open diagonal grid: blocks made using strips of various widths and fiber contents, such as satins and cottons, prints, and patterns

Wonky grid on a photo of crocus

Inspiration photo by Pat Busby

Spring Frost by Pat Busby, 44″ × 34″, 2016

Wonky grid: blocks made using strips of various widths and fabrics, including cottons and satins in prints and solids

CUTTING, SORTING, AND ORGANIZING STRIPS

When making Log Cabin quilts, it pays to cut efficiently and organize your strips so you can find them when you need them. It's all about the strips, cutting them carefully, and organizing them.

CUTTING TOOLS

- Rotary cutter (A 60mm blade is recommended.)
- Acrylic rotary cutting ruler
- Large gridded cutting mat
- Steam iron

CUTTING TECHNIQUE

You can cut the strips any way you are comfortable, but I like to cut multiple strips at one time.

1. Place the fabric long ways on the ironing board and iron it flat.

2. Place the next piece on top, matching the raw edge, and iron again. Repeat this step for 6–8 layers of fabric.

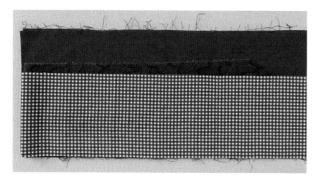
Layers of fabric ironed and ready for cutting

3. Move the fabrics to the cutting mat. Cut the fabrics with an acrylic ruler and rotary cutter.

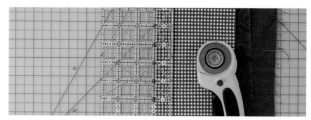
Line up the ruler with the matching raw sides of the layered fabrics.

STRIP SIZES

Strips can be cut all the same width for an even look to the quilt or different widths for a varied design. When using same-width strips, I recommend 1½˝ strips. For different strip widths, use 1˝ and 1¼˝ strips with the 1½˝ strips.

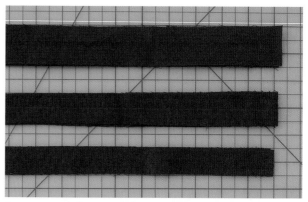
Recommended strip widths: 1˝, 1¼˝, and 1½˝

Look through the book at all the wonderful Artful Log Cabins my students and I have made. Each caption describes the type of strips used—either all the same width or various widths. This will help with your decision.

SORTING AND ORGANIZING STRIPS

It is important to stay somewhat organized when you have strips in all colors and values. Only you know what will work best for you, but here are some ideas. I generally organize by color rather than width.

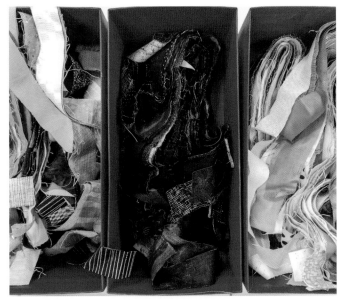

Shoeboxes

Plastic boxes

Plastic boxes with lengthwise dividers

Drying rack

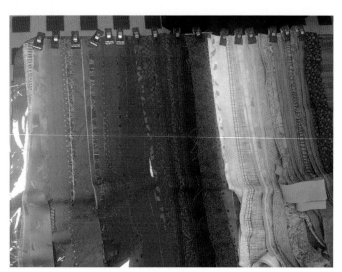

Binder/bulldog clips or binding clips and a board

Safety pins and binder rings: Pin the ends of like-color or like-value strips together, slide onto binder rings, and hang on a nail or hook. To straighten up at the end of the day, just give them a shake!

ENLARGING THE GRID

Refer to Grids (page 14).

The chosen grid will need to be enlarged to the full size of the quilt.

ENLARGING AN EVEN PERPENDICULAR GRID

When using an even perpendicular grid, the percentage of enlargement needs to be determined.

For example, if the original grid has 1½″ × 1½″ squares and the grid has 6 blocks across and 8 blocks down, here are three possibilities:

At a 300% enlargement, the finished block is 4½″ × 4½″, and the finished quilt will be 27″ × 36″.

At a 400% enlargement, the finished block is 6″ × 6″, and the finished quilt will be 36″ × 48″.

At a 500% enlargement, the finished block is 7½″ × 7½″, and the finished quilt will be 45″ × 60″.

It all depends on the size of the finished quilt you desire.

ENLARGING ALL OTHER GRIDS

Diagonal, Even, Diamond, Open, Variable, Wonky, and Radiating Grids

When enlarging the other grids, you'll need to take a different approach.

MATHEMATICAL GRID ENLARGEMENT

1. Decide about how big you want the quilt to be.

2. Measure the height or width of your original grid. As an example, we'll use measurements of 6″ × 8″.

3. If you don't need to make the quilt a specific size, you can use an easy trial-and-error method: Multiply 1 side of the grid by 200% (6″ × 2 = 12″).

If that's not suitable, keep trying different percentages until you get to a size that works for you. For example, if you want the quilt to be about 30″ wide, you'll use 500% for your enlargement (6″ × 5 = 30″). Your final quilt will be 30″ × 40″.

4. Take the original acetate grid drawing, taped to a piece of clean white paper, to a print shop and have 3 enlarged copies made—one to pin on your design wall to use as a guide, one to cut apart into finished-size templates for making the blocks, and an extra copy just to have in case you misplace a block in the process.

USING A PROPORTION SCALE

Using a proportion scale is an easy way to determine what percentage to enlarge a grid. There are two wheels on the proportion scale. The small wheel relates to the size of the small grid; the large wheel relates to the size of the large quilt. The tool makes it easy. Just follow these steps:

1. Measure 1 side of the grid. For this example, it is 8″. Find 8″ on the small wheel and hold it with your finger.

2. How long do you want that side of your quilt to be? If the finished size needs to be 35″, roll the small wheel around until the 8″ mark is below the 35″ mark on the large wheel.

3. The wheel is set. Look into the window on the small wheel where it says "percentage of original size." The arrow points to 440%; that is the percentage of enlargement. Ask the copy shop to set the copier to 440% to get the proper size.

4. You can also check to see what the other dimension of your quilt will be. Measure the other side of the grid. For this example, the grid is 8″ × 12″. Without moving the wheel, find 12″ on the small wheel and look to see the measurement on the large wheel. At 440%, the other side of your quilt will be 53″. An 8″ × 12″ grid enlarged by 440% will result in a 35″ × 53″ quilt.

Many larger print shops can make copies up to 36″ wide. If you design will be larger than 36″, it will be enlarged in 36″-wide strips that can be taped together to create the whole grid.

tip   *If you are aiming for a specific size, use a proportion scale.*

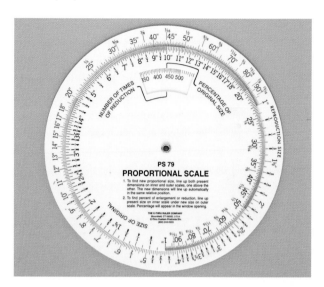

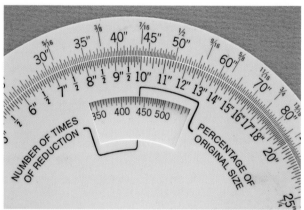

Proportion scale

ENLARGING ONE BLOCK AT A TIME

This method enlarges one block at a time, so you can start working on your piece before going to the print shop for enlargement of the whole grid. This method works when using a whole percentage for enlarging the grid, such as 300% or 400%.

1. Determine the percentage you want to enlarge the grid. Make a copy of the grid at the original size. From the copy, cut out the block you want to work on. This cutout is your template for enlarging the block—it is also the template for the center of that block!

2. A large piece of paper is needed for drawing the enlargement. Draw a line across the paper approximately ½″ above the bottom edge.

3. Align the bottom edge of the template on the left end of the drawn line. Place a ruler along the left edge of the template and draw a line extending from the left side of the template to the top of the paper.

4. Make a mark on the bottom line at the lower right corner of the template.

Steps 1–4

5. Shift the template to the right, aligning the bottom left template corner with the mark you made in Step 4. Make another mark on the bottom line at the lower right corner of the template. Shift the template to the right a second time, aligning the bottom left corner with the last mark you made. In this example, the block is enlarged 300% by marking the template 3 times. If you want the block 400% bigger, mark the template 4 times, and so on.

6. Place a ruler along the right side of the template and draw a line extending from the right side of the template to the top of the paper.

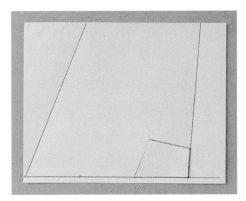

Steps 5 and 6

7. Make a mark on the drawn line at the top right corner of the template.

8. Shift the template up the line on the right, aligning the lower right corner of the template with the mark from Step 7. Make a mark at the top right corner of the template on the drawn line. Shift the template a second time, aligning the bottom right corner with the last mark you made. The template has been marked 3 times along the bottom edge and 3 times on the right edge to enlarge the block 300%.

9. Place a ruler along the top edge of the template and draw a line to meet the drawn line on the left side of the page. The block has been enlarged. This will be the finished size of that block.

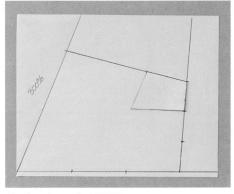

Block enlarged at 300%

BLOCK
CONSTRUCTION

Refer to Grids (page 14).

Place an enlarged copy of the grid on a design wall, and put the acetate grid drawing back on the inspiration photo. Choose a starting block—it can be anywhere. I like to use sticky notes to border the block I am working on and then move the sticky notes as I go from block to block, keeping me focused on the one block.

Use sticky notes to organize the process of making the blocks.

Look at the beginning block to determine the proportion of color needed. Locate the corresponding block on the enlarged grid copy. This is the finished block size that you will be constructing. Cut this out for reference. If you have enlarged one block as described in Enlarging One Block at a Time (page 40), that enlarged block will be your reference.

Some students prefer to label the grid with a number for each block to make it easier when they start making the blocks. You can start in the upper left corner with 1 and work across and then back to the left until all the blocks have numbers.

Remember that you are not trying to re-create your inspiration so that a flower looks like a flower or a house looks like a house. You are creating an abstraction. The colors in a particular block don't necessarily have to be in corresponding positions, just a close approximation of the proportion of the colors in the block. So if a part of the image in that block has a tiny bit of white, a lot of blue, and a medium amount of green, pull your strips in that proportion. Use those colors to make up the block. You will be surprised how not having to worry about exact placement and just working with the proportion of color will result in a fantastic Artful Log Cabin—but you have to trust yourself and the photo.

CONSTRUCTING BLOCKS WITH EVEN GRIDS

Perpendicular, Diagonal, and Diamond Grids

USING STRIPS OF THE SAME WIDTH

Using fabric strips of the same width is the easiest way to construct a block, because only color and value need to be determined—not strip width. I recommend this if you are a beginner.

1. Set the machine to a straight stitch and move the needle over to the far right. A small seam allowance is good because these are wall quilts and you don't need the standard ¼˝ seam allowance.

2. For the block center, cut a square from one of the strips for the even perpendicular and diagonal grids. For the diamond grid, the center "square" will be a smaller diamond (the size it is in the grid drawing).

3. Sew a strip to the square (or diamond). Press the seam away from the center square (or diamond). Then cut off the strip tail even with the square (or diamond). This is the block center with the first log.

4. Working in a clockwise direction, sew the next strip to the unit, pressing the seam allowance toward the new strip and then cutting off the strip tail.

5. Sew around and around until the block is at least a ¼˝ larger than the finished block size. Keep the template next to your sewing area to use as a guide.

6. Square up the block, referring to Squaring Even Blocks (page 54). All the blocks will be trimmed to the same size for the even grids.

Even perpendicular grid on a photo of a giraffe

Inspiration photo by Carolyn Bennett

A Higher Point of View by Carolyn Bennett, 40˝ × 32˝, 2016

Even perpendicular grid: blocks made using strips of the same width

Random grid on a photo of a winter scene

Inspiration photo by John Gavrilis

Winter Scene by Jody L. DeCoursin-Good, 22″ × 26″, 2015

Random grid: blocks made using strips of the same width

 Using Strips of Various Widths

With fabric strips of various widths, you have another choice other than color and value. Now you have to decide which strip width to use. I don't really think about it much; I just pull from my containers and let things happen. Sometimes as I get close to the finished size for the block, I may decide to use a thinner strip if I am close or a wider strip if I am short. Sometimes I have to add an extra strip to one side or another, but it really doesn't matter in the end.

CONSTRUCTING BLOCKS WITH ALL OTHER GRIDS

Random, Open, Variable, Wonky, and Radiating Grids

1. Cut the beginning block from the enlarged copy to keep by the machine as a template for the finished size. Cut out the corresponding block from the original (unenlarged) copy of the grid. This is the template for the center of the pieced block.

2. Place the small template on the fabric that you want to use for the block center and cut the fabric piece about a ¼″ bigger all around. Notice how the original center template is a smaller proportion of the enlarged block.

3. Set the machine to a straight stitch and move the needle over to the far right. A small seam allowance is good because these are wall quilts and you don't need the standard ¼″ seam allowance.

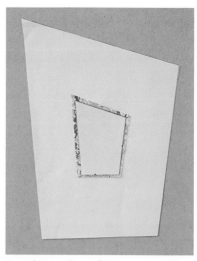

Template with cut fabric centered on the enlarged block

4. Sew a strip to one side of the block center. Press the seam away from the block center. Then cut off the strip tail even with the block center. This is the block center with the first log.

5. Working in a clockwise direction, sew the next strip, pressing the seam allowance toward the new strip and then cutting off the strip tail.

6. As the block gets bigger, you can place it on the template to determine when the fabric block is about a ¼˝ larger on all sides of the template.

7. Square up the block, referring to Squaring Wonky or Irregular Blocks (page 55).

 Sometimes with the wonky grid, you need to add more strips to one side or another—perhaps randomly adding two strips to one side and then moving around. Or you can make a little pattern with strips or checkerboards to add something different. Look to your photograph for suggestions of what to do.

Addition of strips to bring the wonky block out to full size

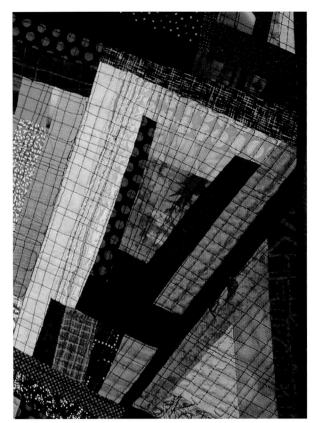

Additions may be needed to fill in.

EXAMPLES USING STRIPS OF THE SAME WIDTH

Wonky grid on photo of water lilies

Photo courtesy of PhotoSpin.com/Mei-Ling Tsao

Sleeping on the Lake by Avis Hayden, 21″ × 27″ each, 2015

Wonky grid: blocks made using strips of the same width. Two quilts were created to make a diptych.

Wonky grid on a photo of a canyon

Inspiration photo by Adriel Heisey

Colorful Canyon by Jody L. DeCoursin-Good, 22˝ × 32˝, 2015

Wonky grid: blocks made using strips of the same width

EXAMPLES USING STRIPS OF VARIOUS WIDTHS

Wonky grid on a photo of autumn trees by the lake

Inspiration photo by Lisa Steinka

Autumn at the Lake—Sweet Memory by Lisa Steinka, 20˝ × 33˝, 2016

Wonky grid: blocks made with strips of various widths

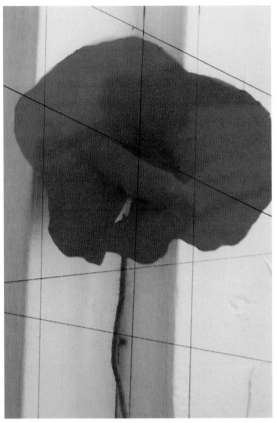

Wonky grid on a photo of a poppy

Inspiration photo by Steve Hamlin

Sisters Poppy by Lisa E. Pries-Linn, 27″ × 33″, 2016

Wonky grid: blocks made using strips of various widths

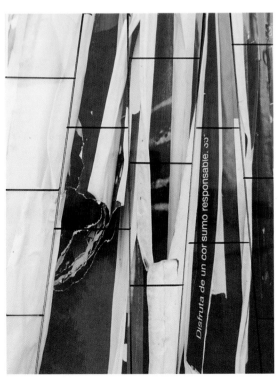

Wonky grid on a photo of posters layered on a wall

Inspiration photo by Katie Pasquini Masopust

Days of Wine and Roses by Katie Pasquini Masopust, 31″ × 39″, 2014

Wonky grid: blocks made using strips of various widths

CABBAGE ROSE BLOCKS

Cabbage Rose blocks are a variation of the straight-line Log Cabin block. They appear to be round until you square them off. It is fun to randomly use this block to add a little bit of movement and variety to any grid layout.

To create the Cabbage Rose block, start with the center square and sew the first round as you would a regular block. Then start to shift the strips—instead of four strips to go around, there will be five. For the next round, it might take six or seven strips to make it around. Try not to have any strips parallel to the strip beside it. Stop when the block is larger than the desired finished size. Learn how to square up the blocks in Squaring Wonky or Irregular Blocks (page 55).

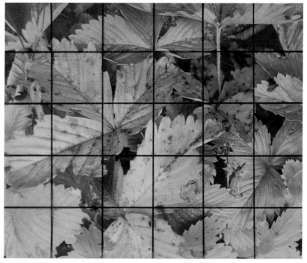

Even perpendicular grid on a photo of strawberry leaves

Inspiration photo by Katie Pasquini Masopust

Cabbage Rose block before it is squared up

Cabbage Rose blocks are most often used in combination with other blocks.

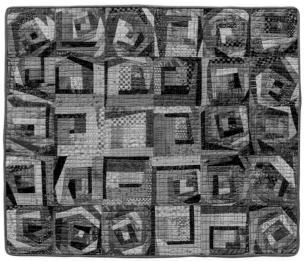

Autumn Leaves by Katie Pasquini Masopust, 23″ × 28″, 2014

Even perpendicular grid: blocks made using strips of various widths. Orange strips make the Log Cabin blocks, and green strips make the Cabbage Rose blocks.

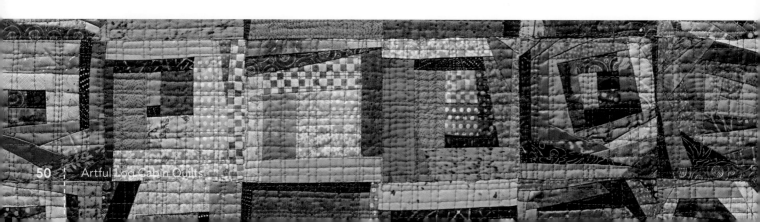

Open grid on a digitally manipulated collage

Inspiration image by Donna Dynes

Wonkiness Complement by Donna Dynes, 24″ × 26″, 2015

Open grid: Log Cabins and Cabbage Roses with strips of various widths

CIRCULAR BLOCKS

The circular block is a great way to get a curved look while using only straight strips. I call it a Circular Log Cabin. Creating the circle effect requires four units. Construct the units the same as a traditional Log Cabin with only one difference: One side, either the dark or light, is made with thin 1˝ strips, and the other side (the opposite value) is made with wide 1½˝ or 2˝ strips. Value is very important. Keep the wide strips and the thin strips in different values or colors from each other to get the circle to appear; then put four units together to create the circular effect.

With the thick strips of orange and the thin strips of green, this traditional quilt block creates an orange circle that is clear and easy to see.

The yellow values are too close between the thin and thick strips.

In this block of thin black strips and thick black strips, the curved pattern is not noticeable.

The circle is apparent in these blocks because of the contrasting values between the thin and thick strips.

Even perpendicular grid on a photo of a Grenada sunset

Inspiration photo by Katie Pasquini Masopust

Grenada Sunset by Katie Pasquini Masopust, 36″ × 36″, 2015

Even perpendicular grid: blocks made using strips of various widths

the proof is in the value

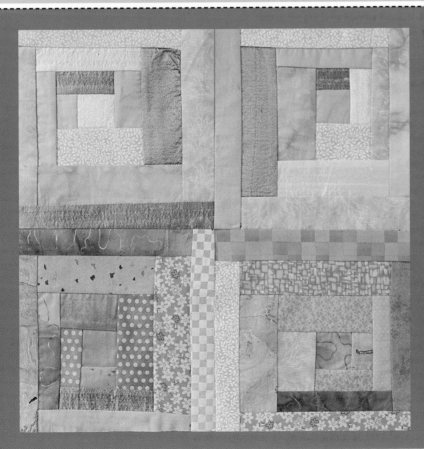

In case you didn't believe me, these blocks don't show the circle because the thin and thick strips are the same value, proving that the saying "color gets all the credit, but value does all the work" is correct!

SQUARING UP
THE BLOCKS

There are several ways to square or straighten blocks after they have been constructed.

SQUARING EVEN BLOCKS

USE A GRIDDED CUTTING MAT

1. Draw the size of the block with the seam allowance directly on a cutting mat. Extend the lines beyond the block area so you can see them after covering them with the fabric block.

tip I use a permanent marker to mark the block size on the mat, as the marks don't smudge and it's a block size I'll use over and over.

2. Place the block on the mat over the lines. With a rotary cutter and ruler, cut off whatever is outside the drawn lines.

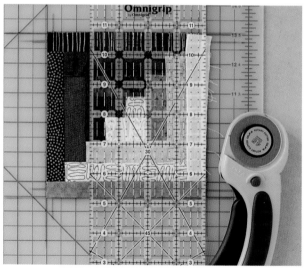

Using the gridded mat

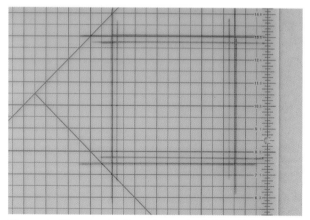

The mat with red guidelines shows the finished block size plus the seam allowance.

USE A SQUARE TEMPLATE OR RULER

Make a square template or use a square ruler that is ½˝ larger than the block's finished size. Place the ruler or template on top of the block, and use a rotary cutter to cut off the excess.

Using a square template to square up a block

SQUARING WONKY OR IRREGULAR BLOCKS

1. Place the cut-out enlarged template on the back of the fabric block, and mark at the corners using a pencil that will leave visible marks.

2. Using a ruler, draw the lines between the corner marks to indicate the sewing line.

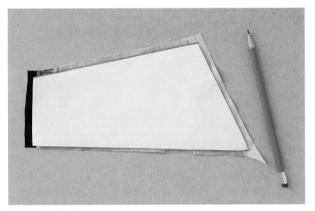

Mark the block corners.

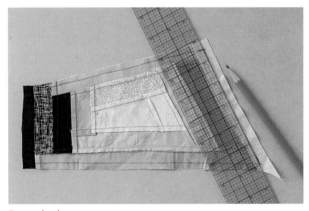

Draw the lines.

---

3. Use a ruler and rotary cutter to add the ¼˝ seam allowance beyond the drawn line; cut off the excess.

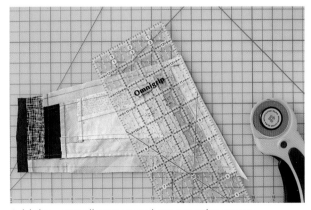

Add the seam allowance and cut away the excess.

QUILT
CONSTRUCTION

PUTTING THE BLOCKS TOGETHER

After all the blocks are made and squared up, pin them to a design wall so the entire quilt can be seen. If the blocks are all the same size, you can move them around to make a better composition of color or value. At this point, it isn't important to stay true to the inspirational photograph. If the piece will look better with a few of the blocks rearranged, then by all means, move them around.

Wonky or irregular-sized blocks are all different sizes. If you want to change something, you will have to remake the block.

Sew the blocks together using a ¼˝ seam allowance for square blocks or the drawn sewing line for wonky and irregular blocks.

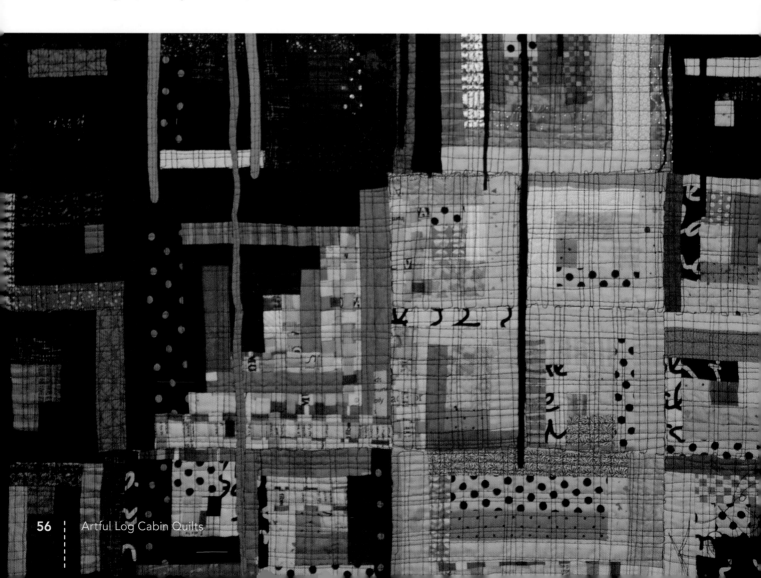

ARTFUL LOG CABINS AS A BACKGROUND FOR APPLIQUÉ

Artful Log Cabin quilt tops can be used as a background for appliqué to create a many-layered piece. Appliqué anything on the surface.

Open grid on a photo of a street in Japan

Inspiration photo by Katie Pasquini Masopust

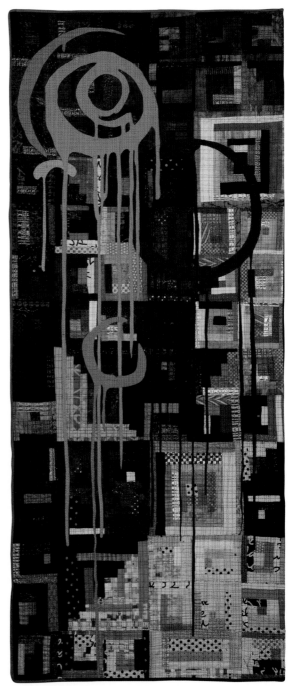

Japan Streets by Katie Pasquini Masopust, 55″ × 24″, 2014

Open grid: blocks made using strips of various widths. The pieced background is used as a background for appliquéd graffiti shapes.

Photo by Carolyn Wright

Random grid on a photo of a garden in Managua, Nicaragua

Inspiration photo by Jomama Van Loo

Traditions by Jomama Van Loo, 24˝ × 22˝, 2015

Random grid: blocks made using strips of various widths. The pieced background is used as a background for appliquéd flowers.

QUILTING

There are as many possibilities for quilting as there are quilts.
The following are a few of the quilting ideas I like to use.

Sampler of quilting patterns: The upper left section has a different quilting design in each strip; the upper right is overall meandering or stipple quilting. The lower left is an allover grid, and the lower right is a spiral starting in the center and moving out to the edge of the block.

FILL PATTERNS

Each strip is quilted with a different fill-in pattern that can be either random or suggested by the fabric print.

Wonky grid on a photo of a rose

Inspiration photo by Katie Pasquini Masopust

A Rose Is a Rose by Katie Pasquini Masopust, 28″ × 21″, 2014

Wonky grid: blocks made using strips of the same width. This quilt was quilted with a different pattern in each strip, and the thread color matches the fabric.

Detail of *A Rose Is a Rose*

GRID QUILTING

A grid of horizontal and vertical lines over each block creates even more grids and adds texture.

Wonky grid on a photo of industrial kitchen utensils

Inspiration photo by Katie Pasquini Masopust

Spoons and Whisks by Katie Pasquini Masopust, 30″ × 24″, 2014

Wonky grid: blocks made using strips of various widths. This quilt was quilted with a grid in each block.

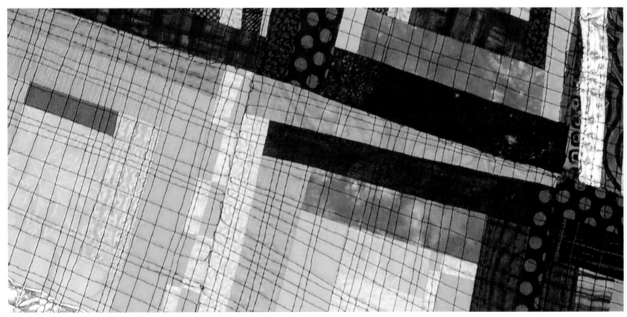

Detail of *Spoons and Whisks*

SPIRAL QUILTING

Spiral quilting that moves out from the center of the square adds movement.

Detail of *Bromeliad* by Katie Pasquini Masopust (See the full quilt and inspiration photo in Grids, page 21.)

OTHER QUILTING PATTERNS

Take some time to think about quilting your Artful Log Cabin quilt top. For example, if your inspiration photo is of a flower, consider quilting the essence of the flower lines on the pieced Log Cabin blocks. Or use various textures in the areas that cross over the seamlines. Following are some quilting examples of student work.

Even perpendicular grid on a photo of an old farm wheel against a wall

Inspiration photo by Becky Poisson

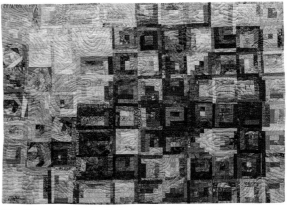

The Wheel by Becky Poisson, 32″ × 45″, 2015

Even perpendicular grid: blocks made using strips of various widths. This quilt was quilted with a pattern that looks similar to wood grain.

COMBINING QUILTING PATTERNS

Of course, there is no reason you can't combine quilting patterns
and motifs in any way that works for your quilt.

Wonky grid on a photo of candy

Inspiration photo by Susan Costantino

Licorice … Yum! by Susan Costantino, 30″ × 24″, 2016

Wonky grid: blocks made using strips of various widths.
This quilt was quilted with a combination of spiral and
straight-line quilting.

Detail of Licorice … Yum!

Wonky grid on a collage

Inspiration image by Donna Dynes

Wonkiness by Donna Dynes, 24″ × 26″, 2015

Wonky grid: blocks made using strips of various widths. This quilt was quilted with a combination of spiral and grid quilting.

Detail of *Wonkiness*

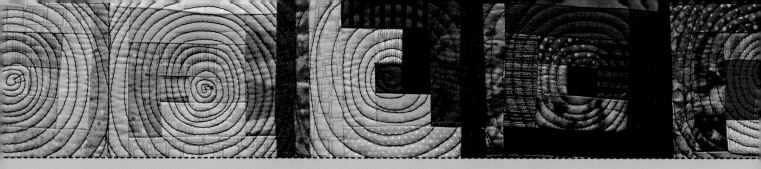

FINISHING

BLOCKING THE QUILT

The finished piece must be square or true to the shape intended. The quilt should be blocked so it will lie flat.

1. Place the quilt on a flat surface.

2. Steam the entire surface with a steamer. You can use a professional steamer, like the ones used to steam clothes in a dress shop, or an iron that has a steam setting. Start in the center and work out in circles to the outside edge.

3. Let the quilt dry overnight before moving it.

SQUARING THE QUILT

Squaring usually means trimming the edges of the quilt so the corners are 90°, or true right angles. Because some of these quilts are not square, "squaring the shape" means trimming the edges straight as needed.

1. Move the blocked quilt to a large rotary cutting mat.

2. For a quilt with 90° corners, use a T-square to line up the corners and trim away anything outside the desired edge. For a quilt without 90° corners, use a ruler and rotary cutter to trim the straight sides of the quilt.

MAKING A SLEEVE

If your quilt is square or rectangular, a simple sleeve running along the top edge, through which a rod can be put, is the easiest way to display a quilt on a wall.

Follow these steps to make a hanging sleeve:

1. Cut a strip of fabric 9″ wide by the length of the quilt's top edge.

2. Turn under the 2 short edges about ½″ and stitch. This ensures that the ends won't get caught in the binding on the sides of the quilt when the binding is sewn to the quilt.

3. Fold the sleeve in half, with the right side out, and pin the unturned edges of the sleeve to the top edge of the quilt, matching the raw edges. These edges will be stitched into the binding.

4. Hand stitch the folded edge to the back of the quilt.

MAKING A LABEL

Use your inspiration photo or painting to create a label. If you are comfortable using a computer, there are many ways to print on fabric using an inkjet printer. The following is another way to create a label.

1. Place the inspiration image on a piece of white paper.

2. Write the quilt title, the quilt size, the date it was completed, and your name, city, and state on the paper.

3. Transfer the image to white fabric using a photo-transfer technique. You may have to reduce the image when transferring it to make the label a manageable size.

4. Pin the label to the lower right side of the quilt back. The outer edges will be stitched into the binding. Hand stitch the remaining edges of the label.

WRITING OR PRINTING YOUR OWN LABELS

You can write your own label on fabric with a permanent Pigma Micron pen, or you can print your own labels using an inkjet printer and pretreated fabric sheets. Follow the manufacturer's instructions on the package of pretreated fabric sheets.

Add a label.

BINDING THE QUILT

Binding will finish the quilt's raw outside edge.

1. From the binding fabric, cut enough 1¾″-wide bias strips to go around the perimeter of the quilt, plus extra for turning corners.

2. Sew these strips together with diagonal seams to make a long strip.

3. Press the strip in half lengthwise, right side out. Using a ¼″ seam, machine stitch the binding to the front of the quilt, right sides together and with the raw edges even with the quilt edge. Be sure to catch the sleeve and label in the ¼″ seam.

(A label can also be added *after* binding the quilt by hand sewing the label to the quilt back.) Sew the straight edge along the side of the quilt; when you get to the corner, stop and leave the needle down in the fabric. Pivot the quilt and turn the binding to follow along the next side. I do not miter my corners.

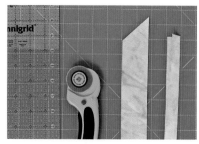
Cut 1¾″ bias strips and fold in half lengthwise.

4. Roll the folded edge of the binding to the back of the quilt and blind stitch in place by hand. I ease the corners around to get a nice smooth curve. Stitch in place.

Finished hanging sleeve, label, and binding

DOCUMENTING THE QUILT

The final stage of the process is to document all that you have done. This is especially important if you plan to enter your art quilt into a competition. Have the finished quilt photographed by a professional photographer. Have digital images made in JPEG (.jpg) versions for emailing and TIF (.tif) versions for reproduction in print.

PHOTOGRAPHY PERMISSIONS

Even if you don't know how the photography of your finished quilt might be used, be sure to get a signed statement from the photographer giving you the right to use the images as you choose, including submitting them for publication. Unless you do this and have the statement in writing, the photographer legally owns the copyright to the photographic images.

Keep a file of your work that includes the date you finished the quilt, the size, and the title. Keep notes on the techniques used and your inspiration. This will make it easy to fill out forms and answer requests when entering your work in shows or for publication.

Wonky grid on a photo of a house

Inspiration photo by Barbara Sklar

Eden House, Key West by Barbara Sklar, 30″ × 20″, 2016

Wonky grid: blocks made using strips of various widths

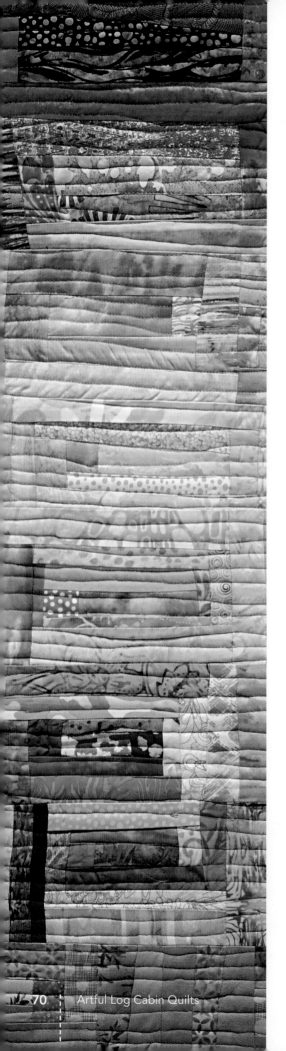

Random grid on a still life painting

Inspiration painting by Jeanne Sellers

Farmer's Market by Jeanne Sellers, 29″ × 28″, 2016

Random grid: blocks made using strips of various widths

Wonky grid on a photo of echinacea flowers

Inspiration photo by Maggie Farmer

I Thought I Was an Echinacea by Maggie Farmer, 37˝ × 50˝, 2016

Wonky grid: blocks made using strips of various widths

Wonky grid on a photo of rusty cans

Inspiration photo by Katie Pasquini Masopust

Trashique by Katie Pasquini Masopust, 39″ × 29″, 2016

Wonky grid: made using strips of various widths

Photo by Carolyn Wright

Wonky grid on a photo of azaleas

Inspiration photo by Helen Walker

Artful Azaleas by Helen Walker, 22″ × 28″, 2016

Wonky grid: blocks made using strips of the same width

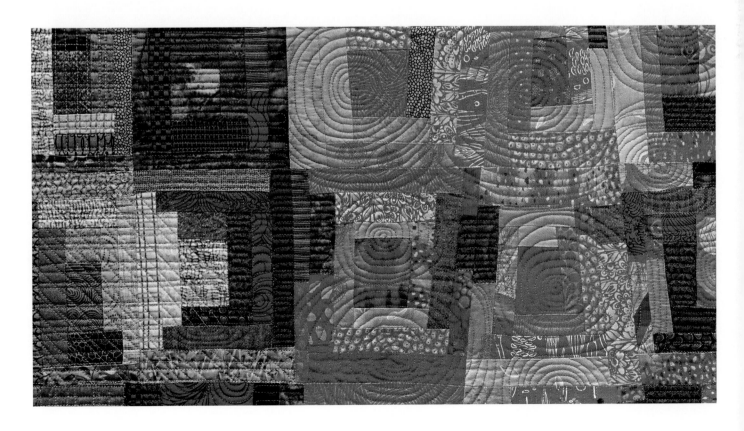

Wonky grid on a photo of a malachite kingfisher

Inspiration photo by Jan Avent

Malachite Kingfisher by Jan Avent, 32″ × 26″, 2015

Wonky grid: blocks made using strips of various widths

Wonky grid on a photo of the old Fox Theatre

Inspiration photo by Judy Shelton

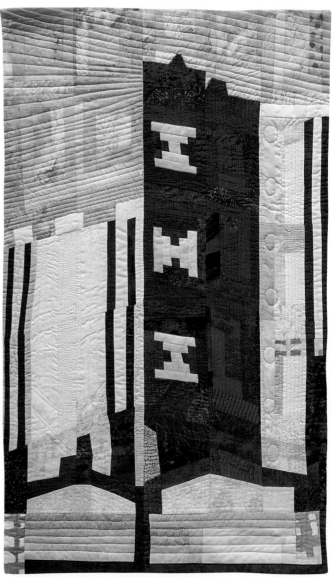

Fox Theatre, Salinas, California by Judy Shelton, 21″ × 35″, 2016

Wonky grid: blocks made using strips of various widths

Wonky grid on a photo of blooming prickly pear cactus

Inspiration photo by Kristi Leduc

PRICKLY apPEARance by Kristi Leduc, 22″ × 29″, 2016

Wonky grid: blocks made using strips of various widths

Open grid on daylilies

Inspiration photo by Jaime Chapin Miller

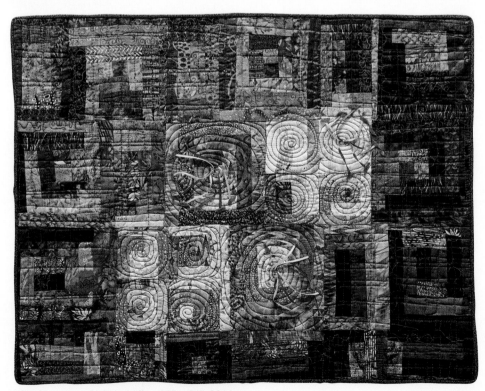

Lilies by Jaime Chapin Miller, 27″ × 21″, 2016

Open grid: blocks made with same width strips

Wonky grid on a photo of tiger lilies

Inspiration photo by Steve Lieske

Tiger Lilies in the Sierras by Sandy Lieske, 21″ × 30″, 2016

Wonky grid: blocks made using strips of various widths

ABOUT THE
AUTHOR

For nearly 30 years, Katie Pasquini Masopust has created high-quality contemporary art quilts that have been coveted and collected by a broad range of admirers. From her early beginnings as a painter dabbling in traditional quiltmaking, her work has evolved from structured mandalas and mind-blowing dimensional pieces to very painterly landscapes executed with the finest fabrics and most creative stitching techniques. Katie's easy, energetic manner has made her a very popular teacher and lecturer.

When not in residence at her studio in Northern California, she travels, presenting her contemporary quilting theories and techniques to classes in North America, Europe, Asia, Australia, and New Zealand.

Katie has been making Log Cabin quilts for many years as a break from her large art quilts. She began transforming traditional Log Cabin quilts into abstract art quilts by using artistic considerations of color and composition based on an inspirational photograph. She now shares her techniques with her students worldwide.

Want even more creative content?

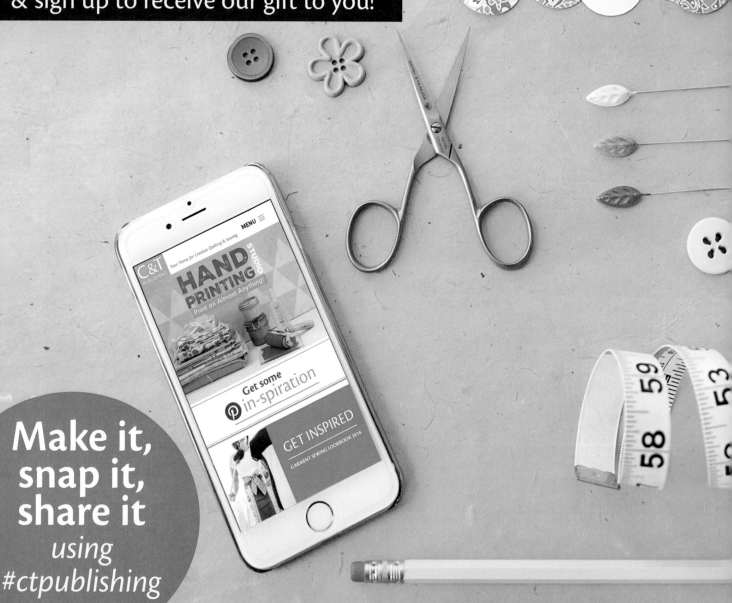

Make it, snap it, share it *using* *#ctpublishing*